CW01494968

www.tastnatur.com

Contents

Re-thinking the Garden

Gardening usually involves growing fruit and vegetables to eat, flowers for their beauty and a constant fight to eradicate weeds! This book aims to help you re-think your garden, as the Edible Garden takes you beyond the vegetable patch.

The easiest way to incorporate this newly discovered source of food is actually to substitute them into your normal recipes. So perhaps replace kale or spring cabbage in stir fries with young dandelion leaves. Try young nettle leaves instead of spinach, and pickle daisy flowers to use instead of capers. Perhaps some clover leaves on a salad as an alternative to cress.

Re-defining Weeds

Weeds are just plants that are in the wrong place or not wanted, so if when we start using them then they gain a purpose in our gardens. Many weeds have nutritional and flavour value, and as any gardener appreciates can grow naturally and abundantly! So if you're going to be weeding the garden anyway, why not try harnessing some of nature's most common plants into your food? Consider assigning designated areas, where certain 'weeds' grow well naturally, and treat them as any other crop.

Re-imagining Flowers

Many flowers are grown in our garden purely for their aesthetic beauty. When we do experience them out of the flower bed or vase, it's likely as a scent such as lavender or rose. However, flowers, although they may not have many nutritional values, do make beautiful and flavourful additions to dishes.

A Note of Caution

When it comes to using plants we don't normally use in our diet it's important to be careful. Plants can be classed as edible, inedible or toxic. Some plants have no nutritional or flavour value, so while they won't harm us, neither will they benefit us in any way. Toxic plants may cause some physical harm or upset. Paradoxically, some plants may be toxic uncooked, yet perfectly edible when processed in some way. Some plants can only really be eaten without causing physical upset at a certain time of year or stage in their life cycle. Edible plants are the ones we can benefit from nutritionally or enjoy their flavour, when used at the right time, in the right way. To ensure these recipes are as useable as possible, I will stick to weeds and flowers that are common to our gardens and therefore most people will recognise, even from childhood. I will also give some guidance on when to use them and how to prepare them. The recipes in this book are based on an electric oven, so reduce the cooking time or temperature for a fan oven (usually about 20°C less).

The important thing with weeds and flowers, as with any food is, if in doubt it's best not to eat it. Choose weeds and flowers that have not been sprayed with pesticides or weed killer and are safe for consumption.

Before using plants think about whether they're free from pesticides and whether any animals have been using the area where they grow.

Preparing and Using Plants

Check whether they are edible and that it's the right time of year to use them.

Once you're confident that the plant is ready to eat, make sure they're washed thoroughly and prepared before using them.

Experiment with weeds and flowers and find which ones work to add or substitute into your favourite recipes. Using recipes you're familiar with should help build up confidence in which flowers and weeds compliment other flavours. Try them fresh and dried to compare. The ratio of using dried herbs instead of fresh is about one to three, so keep this in mind when adjusting your recipes.

Daisies

The daisy is actually two flowers in one - the white petals count as one flower and the centre, formed of tiny yellow disc petals, is technically another. It's closely related to artichoke and is a very nutritious plant. Daisies have also been used for their medicinal properties throughout history, and Roman military doctors would soak bandages with daisy juices and use them to bind their soldiers' wounds. All of the daisy is edible and can be used fresh or dried.

Collect the flowers when they're open during the day to make teas or for using as a herb, or collect shut at first thing or at evening if you want to use them to pickle instead of capers. To dry the flowers for tea, cut them just under the flower head and then wash and dry. Place evenly onto a sheet of kitchen paper, ensure individual flowers aren't touching, and there's plently of dry air circulating around the area. They should dry in a week, but keep checking and turning them to ensure they don't develop mould or mildew. Once completely dry, store in an airtight container, in a cool and dark place.

Daisy leaves can be used either cooked or raw.

Ideas:

Try pickling as a substitute for capers on salads. Freeze in the middle of ice cubes and to decorate drinks, such as cocktails.

Dry flowerheads and use as a chamomile-type tea. Use dried leaves and flowers as a herb for recipes such as soups and casseroles.

Nettles

Nettles are rich in vitamins A and C, iron, potassium, manganese, and calcium.

Nettles should be collected in Spring and new young leaves from the top of the plant should be used, and plants that have gone to seed shouldn't be consumed. By cutting the tops of the plants, flowering and seeding is delayed, so two or three crops can be collected from a single plant before letting it go to seed. Nettles are best cooked or blended to neutralise the formic acid. Freezing them will also achieve this, and then they can be used straight in smoothies or recipes.

Wear protective gloves to collect nettles, and pick individual leaves if cooking and using on the day. If drying for tea, you can cut the stem under the new growth, above where another pair of leaves are starting, and tie stems together in small bunches. They can then be hung upside down in a cool, dry area, allowing for plently of air circulation. They should be fully dry in two weeks, but check on them regularly and turn to keep mildew and mould forming. When ready, the sting shouldn't be a problem, but wear gloves if you prefer, and place the dried bunch in a large bowl and crumble and tear the leaves into the bowl, leaving only the stems behind. You can store the nettle leaf mix in an airtight container, in a cool cupboard.

Ideas:

Steam young nettle leaves and use like spinach. Try stirring some cooked leaves into creamy mash potato. Use dried nettle leaves as a herbal tea. They combine well with dried daisy flowers. Wash and freeze leaves to kill the sting and add to smoothies. Try in soups, stir fries or pesto.

Cleavers

Commonly called sticky weed or goosegrass, this plant is usually noticed when the round fruit have become stuck to clothing or a pet's fur and have to be picked off one by one.

Cleavers are known to have cleansing properties, and you can use young shoots or the tip of older plants to make tea. It's a good idea to strain the brew to ensure any hooks are removed before drinking. It's also a great addition to smoothies and soups. It has a high quantity of vitamins, and is rich in minerals such as silica, which is needed for nails, hair and teeth.

The botanical name for Cleavers is Galium, which is the Greek for milk and the curdling property of the leaves has been historically used in cheese making.

Cleavers are in the same Rubiaceae plant family as coffee, and the seeds do make a nice less- caffeinated substitute.

It's best to use the young shoots, and before the plant has formed the sticky round fruit, as there are burrs on them.

Ideas:

Try steaming as a vegetable or adding into soup recipes. Use in stir fries, perhaps with dandelion and nettle leaves. The fruit can be collected, slow roasted and ground, to use as coffee type warm beverage.

Dandelions

Dandelions are mainly out when days and nights are equal in length, so predominantly twice a year mid Spring and mid Autumn. Therefore they are one of the first sources of food for bees in the year, so if you're going to get rid of them using chemicals, leave treating them with weedkiller on them until other flowers are out as well. Of course, treating with chemicals means that they then become inedible.

Dandelion leaves contain vitamins A, C, and K, and are good sources of calcium, potassium, iron, and manganese. Petals, leaves and roots are edible, the stalk or white parts aren't usually used as they are bitter.

Young leaves are the best to use fresh, and can be eaten raw in salads, but cooking does negate the bitterness of older leaves. Dandelion leaves can be collected into small bunches, tied together, and hung upside down in a cool, airy place to dry. They can be cut up and stored, and added to tea mixes or used as a herb.

The petals can be pulled from the flowerhead and sprinkled raw onto salads or dried on kitchen towels for about a week to add to tea mixes. Be prepared to get pollen over and under your nails!

During times when coffee beans were scarce, such as during times of war, different plants were used to make ersatz coffee. Dandelion root can be cleaned, slow roasted until dry and crushed to use as a coffee type drink. The root can also be cooked as a root vegetable, like parsnip. Dandelion roots are sweeter in Spring, before they flower, so are better for eating. During the Autumn they have less sugar and more fiber so will be less sweet, and after flowering they can become woody.

> **Ideas:**
>
> Use young leaves or petals fresh in salads. Use leaves as you would spinach. Try steaming or adding to stir fries and soups. Slow roast until dry and crush the roots to use as a 'coffee'.

Clover

All of the clover plant is edible, from both the red and white clover. The flowers have a nectar quality and can be dried to use for teas or used raw. Likewise, the leaves can be added to salads or soups raw, or spread out evenly over kitchen paper and dried. The dried leaves have a hint of vanilla and are great as a herb or added to tea mixes. Even the cooked root is edible.

Store dried flowers and leaves in an airtight container, in a cool, dark cupboard, as you would any other herb.

Ideas:

Use the leaves raw or cooked as a potherb. Young leaves, before flowering are preferable to use in salads or soups, and can also be cooked and used like spinach. Dried seed pods and flowers ground into powder are used as a flour. The dried flowers are best known for making tea. Dried leaves, with their hint of a vanilla aroma, are great as a herb.

Dahlias

Dahlias were initially imported for their tubers, as a food. The Victorians however realised that the flowers were beautiful and started using them in gardens, so we forgot that they're edible. The petals are edible too. The flavour and texture of the tubers varies and depends on the variety and soil, so try researching different ones to see which you prefer. Make sure the dahlias have not been growing anywhere near soil which has been treated or affected by chemicals, as most likely they will be stored in the tuber.

Ideas:

Use the fresh petals to decorate food. Try boiling tubers, ensuring they are soft before eating, or boil them to soften before roasting with some olive oil and seasoning.

Roses

A lot of modern roses don't have perfume, so the rule for using them in food is that if it smells nice, it will taste nice.

Rosehips are also edible, but often aren't left to develop on garden roses, so you're more likely to have these if you have wild roses in your garden. Rosehips have hairs inside, which can cause irritation, and have traditionally been used as itching powder. It's therefore important to get rid of any hairs, for example after boiling to make jelly or syrup. Strain through a very fine muslin.

Ideas:

A great use is to make jelly or syrup from petals or rosehips. Rose petals can be dried and used in herbal teas or added to Earl Grey tea.

Pansies

Multi coloured pansies and viola are available most of the year to brighten up flower beds and hanging baskets, but they are also edible.

Ideas:

Decorate salads or desserts with fresh or crystallised flowers.

Calendula

Also called pot marigold, these striking orange or yellow flowers are decorative, but also make a great herb, and have been referred to as Poor Man's Saffron.

The petals can be used fresh or dried on kitchen paper and stored in an air-tight container as a herb.

Ideas:

Use as a herb and add fresh or dried, to soups, casseroles etc. Dry the petals and use as a herbal tea. Sprinkle fresh petals on salads.

Carnations

This is a popular flower as an addition to bouquets, however the petals are edible, and as they come in a variety of colours and make great decoration for desserts.

Ideas:

Pluck the fresh petals to use as an edible decoration, and avoid the white bit under the flower, as it is bitter.

Lavender

Many know or have used lavender for the smell, but many don't realise that it's edible too. Lavender flowers and leaves can be used dry or fresh.

Cut lavender at the stem just before the flowers open to get the strongest fragrance, but they can be left until later if you want to enjoy them in the garden and use them fresh until later in the Summer. You can cut mature flowers just above the leaves. Tie the stems together in small bunches, so that air can circulate around the flowers to stop mould or mildew developing, and cut the ends so that they are even.

Hang the lavender upside down in a dark area, or at least away from direct sunlight, so the colour fades as little as possible. Ensure that there's plenty of air circulation and that they keep dry. Leave for between a fortnight and a month. Check regularly to see when flowers are dry, when they're ready they should fall off the stem easily.

Once ready, you can the either keep them where they are, or remove the flowers and store them in an airtight container in a cool, dark place.

Ideas:

Lavender leaves are a good subsitute in recipes which use sage for example. Lavender flowers are lovely to have as part of a relaxing herbal tea. Try combining with chocolate mint or lemon balm or add to Earl Grey tea.

Fuchsia

Not only do fuchsia flowers look amazing in the garden, but both flowers and berries are edible and add great colour and flavour to food.

Collect the flowers from below the ovary (green bulbous part) once they're fully open and preferably on a dry day. Discard any with mould or mildew growing on them. Remove the stamen and pistil (the long stalks in the middle of the flower) and use the flower whole (tubes, petals and sepals).

Fuchsia berries are also edible, and taste varies according to your plant, from fruity, to citrus to peppery. They develop at the base of the flowers, which swell and are ready when they are fully swollen, so give when squeezed. Use berries when soft and purple, but not when they are hard. When the berries are ready, the stalks and berries will come off the plant at the slightest touch. Remove the stalk, clean and they are ready to eat.

Ideas:

Flowers look fantastic on salads and desserts. Berries make a lovely jam or can be added to a crumble or tart. Try adding the berries to yogurt, fruit salads or on muesli or porridge.

Ready to eat
Fuchsia berries

Carrot & Daisy Soup

Ingredients:
20g Butter or Margarine
90g (1 small) Leek, sliced
350g (4 medium) Carrots, sliced
200g (4 small) white Potatoes, cubed
20g frozen (½ a cup) or 40g fresh Daisy flower heads
1 Litre Vegetable Stock

Method:
Melt the margarine in a large non-stick pan, and fry the leeks until soft and browned. Add the rest of the ingredients, and bring to the boil. Reduce the heat, and simmer for about 20 minutes, until the potatoes and carrots are soft. Remove from the heat, and allow to cool a little. Then blend the mixture, return to the pan, add salt and pepper to taste if needed, and re-heat and serve.

Nettle Soup

Ingredients:
An average size carrier bag of new growth Nettle leaves, washed
20g Butter or Margarine
½ an Onion, chopped
2 Carrots, chopped
2 small Potatoes, chopped
190ml of Vegetable Stock
Double Cream (Optional)

Method:
Melt some butter into the bottom of a large saucepan and fry the onion until soft and brown. Add the rest of the ingredients into the saucepan, and bring to the boil, then simmer for about 20 minutes or until the potatoes and carrots have softened. Let the mixture cool a little, then blend the ingredients together. Add salt and black pepper to taste if desired. If you'd prefer a creamier soup, stir in some cream at the end, little by little, until you reach the desired consistency.

Parsnip & Calendula Soup

Ingredients:
4 medium Parsnips, peeled and roughly chopped
2 medium Potatoes, peeled and roughly chopped
1 small Red Onion, peeled and roughly chopped
1 teaspoon dried Clover leaves
3 tablespoons Calendula petals – can be used fresh, from frozen or dried
570ml Vegetable Stock (760ml for a thinner soup)
Black Pepper & Salt, to season
20g Butter or Margarine

Method:
Melt the butter in a pan and add the onion, and fry until onion has browned. Add the rest of the ingredients and bring mixture to the boil, then reduce to a simmer. Simmer for about 20 minutes, or until the parsnips and potatoes have completely softened. Remove from the heat and allow to cool. Blend the mixture, and add more seasoning if needed. Store in an air tight container in the fridge to use later, or just re-heat this sweet and herby soup and serve immediately.

Daisy Capers

Ingredients:
Daisy flowers
Apple Cider Vinegar

Method:
Collect daisies when their heads are closed. Place in a sterilised jar with a sprig of rosemary, black pepper and top up with brine or apple cider vinegar until the flowers are completely covered. Leave for 2 weeks before use.

Brine: 19g of sea salt per 4 cups water. Seal jar and leave for 2 weeks in cool place, until mixture has stopped producing bubbles.

Store in the fridge and add daisies to salads, and use the brine or vinegar for cooking.

Weeds Pesto

Ingredients:
25g Nettle (new growth tops are best)
25g mix of Cleavers (new shoots), Clover leaves and Dandelion leaves
(young are recommended)
30g grated Parmesan
30g Seed Mix (Pumpkin, Pine Nuts and Sunflower)
Sea Salt and freshly ground Black Pepper
85ml (approx.) Extra Virgin Olive Oil

Method:
Place the clean cleavers shoots, nettle and dandelion leaves into a food
processor and roughly blend. Add the parmesan, seed mix and seasoning
and blend well. With the motor still running, pour the oil in until the pesto
thickens.
Store in a clean sealed jar in the fridge. Cover with a layer of oil to prevent
it drying out.

Weeds Pesto Bread

Ingredients:
250 g Self-Raising Flour
1 teaspoon Salt
1 teaspoon Sugar
½ teaspoon Bicarbonate of soda (Bi-carb)
1 teaspoon Cream of Tartar or Apple Cider Vinegar
(any vinegar can be used as a substitute or you can use lemon juice)
150-170ml Milk

Method:
Sift the flour into a bowl, add salt, sugar, bi-carb and stir. Add the cream of tartar or vinegar and then gradually stir in enough milk to form a soft dough. Turn out onto a floured board and knead into the desired shape. Brush plenty of weeds pesto over the top. Bake at 200˚C for about 20 -25 minutes, or until has risen and is golden and crisp on top.

Warm, buttered Weeds Pesto Bread with a salad topped with Clover leaves and Daisy Capers

Lavender & Sage Mushrooms

Ingredients:

Flat Mushrooms (As many as you would like to make)
½ teaspoon Lavender flowers per mushroom
½ teaspoon Sage leaves or Lavender leaves per mushroom
Olive Oil, to drizzle
Optional - Black Pepper and Salt to Season

Method:
Clean and prepare the mushrooms and place on an ovenproof tray.
Sprinkle the Lavender flowers, Sage or Lavender leaves over the top.
Season with Salt and Pepper if desired. Drizzle some Olive Oil over the mushrooms.
Place in a pre-heated oven at 180°C, for approximately 15 -20 minutes, until cooked.

Lavender & Sage
Mushroom served with
young
Dandelion leaves

Nettle & Cheese Sausages

Makes 8 Sausages

Ingredients:

400 g (3 medium) white Potatoes, peeled and quartered
20g Olive Spread
140g (1 large) red Onion, finely chopped
20g young Nettle leaves , quite finely chopped
80g Mature Cheddar, grated
20 small fresh Sage leaves, finely chopped
2 medium Eggs
60g Bread crumbs (bought or homemade)
Salt and Black Pepper to season

Method:

Boil the potatoes in water, and when soft enough to push a knife through easily, strain. Add a dash of milk and mash until smooth.

Whilst the potatoes are boiling, melt the olive spread in a frying pan and once melted add the onion, and cook until soft and browned. Add the nettle and sage, and cook until the nettles have wilted.

Separate the egg whites into a container, cover and place in fridge for later. Put the egg yolks into a large bowl and add the mashed potato, cheese and the onion and nettle mixture. Add a pinch of ground salt and pepper to season, and mix thoroughly.

Line a tray with greaseproof paper or foil. Once the mixture is cool enough, take a handful and form into a sausage shape. You should get about 8 sausages about 4 inches in length and 1.5 inches wide.

Once cooled, place in fridge to chill for at least 30 minutes.

Take the sausages and egg white out of the fridge. Whisk the egg white. Cover the bottom of a small plate with the breadcrumbs. Dip the sausages one at a time into the egg mix until well coated, and then roll in the breadcrumbs until completely coated.

The best results come from frying the sausages. Carefully shallow fry using a few millimetres of heated olive oil or vegetable oil in the bottom of a frying pan on a medium heat, and gently cook the sausages for about 5-10 minutes, turning regularly until heated and the coating is a golden brown. Alternatively, you can coat the sausages well in vegetable or olive oil and place on a baking tray, ensuring a space between each. Pre-heat the oven to 200°C and bake in the centre of the oven for 20 minutes. Carefully turn and re-shape a few times during cooking.

Try serving Nettle and Cheese Sausages with a Dandelion petal and Clover leaf topped salad

Dandelion Leaf Quiche

Pre-heat fan oven to 190°C

Ingredients:
1 small onion (about 87g), chopped
3 cups (about 90 g) washed and chopped fresh Dandelion leaves
1 cup (90g) grated Cheddar Cheese
4 medium Eggs
1 cup (237ml) of Milk
Salt and Pepper to taste
400-450g Shortcrust Pastry

Try serving with creamy mashed Potatoes

Method:
Grease a 9 inch deep dish. Roll out shortcrust pastry on a layer of flour (about 10mm in depth) and cover the bottom and sides of the dish, gently pushing into the sides and cutting off any excess from around the rim. Brown the onion in a pan using about 20g melted butter, and then add the fresh dandelion leaves and cook until wilted. Add two thirds (60g) of the cheddar and season with salt and pepper. Once everything is thoroughly mixed and the cheese is melted, spoon into the shortcrust pastry.
Whisk the eggs and milk in a bowl and season a little with salt and pepper, then pour carefully over the mixture in the dish, ensuring they are thoroughly combined with the dandelion and cheese.
Bake on the middle shelf of the oven for about 15 minutes, until a film starts to set on top. Then carefully, so as not to spill the quiche, evenly sprinkle a handful of grated cheddar on to the top, and return to the oven for about 20-25 minutes, or until the quiche is set in the centre. Rest the quiche for 10 minutes before serving.

Dandelion Dolmades

Ingredients:

200g Long Grain Rice (white)
Dandelion leaves; about 4 inches at the widest part
Fresh Mint, 3 tablespoons, finely chopped
Fresh Lemon Balm, 3 tablespoons, finely chopped
Tomato Passata, 4-5 tablespoons (60-75ml)
Vegetable Stock 380ml

Salt, Black Pepper and Paprika (optional) to season
You can vary the filling, so if you're not using lemon balm, you can add a little lemon juice and mint instead.

Method:

Place rice in a non-stick saucepan and add the boiling stock. Simmer and stir frequently for about 5-10 minutes until the stock is absorbed. The rice should be partially cooked. Add the rest of the ingredients and stir. Place a clean dandelion leaf, shiny side down, on a cutting board. Cut the leaf underneath the second pair of lobes, and cut a small part of the stalk (petiole) away, leaving the surrounding leaf. This frees up the lower lobes to better wrap the filling, and in so doing gets rid of the most rigid part of the leaf.

Place a small spoonful of filling onto the bottom of the leaf, above where the cut has been made, and fold the two bottom lobes tightly over the rice, roll upwards and fold in the next set of lobes and keep rolling into a tight package. Place the rolled dandelion dolma in a shallow oven proof dish with the loose top part of the dandelion leaf facing down. Repeat until you have as many dandelion dolmades as you want. Pour water into the bottom of the dish, so that it comes about half way up the dolma.

Cover with kitchen foil and place in a pre-heated oven at 180°C for about an hour.

Any left over rice in the saucepan can either be used to stuff other plants, such as peppers and tomatos as accompaniments to the Dandelion Dolamdes. Otherwise, keep adding water little by little, with rice at a simmer, whilst regularly stirring, as with making a risotto. Do this until the rice has absorbed all the water, and is cooked, and serve on the side.

Serve Dandelion Dolmades drizzled with olive oil. As a starter, they pair well wth a dollop of greek style yogurt with some lemon, black pepper and mint.

Spring Weeds Fried Rice

Ingredients:
2 small Eggs
1 cup or 200g of boiled Rice
A handful or 5-10g of young Cleaver
 leaves and thin shoots, Clover leaves.
A few Lemon Balm leaves (optional)
Salt or Soy Sauce and Pepper or Chilli
powder to season

Method:
Boil the rice and drain thoroughly. Heat a tablespoon of vegetable oil in a frying pan or wok and add the eggs, scrambling until cooked. Add the rice and keep stirring for 5 minutes, then add another drizzle of oil, and the green leaves. Stir and fry until the leaves have wilted and are cooked through. Add the seasoning of choice and stir for another few minutes. Taste and add more seasoning if needed.

If serving with a stir fry, try replacing your usual greens such as kale or spring cabbage with young Dandelion leaves or new growth Nettle leaves.

Dandelion Marmalade

Ingredients:

2 cups Jam Sugar
2 cups Water
4 cups Dandelion petals, with as much of the surrounding green removed as possible, as the green part will affect the colour and tastes quite bitter
2 cups Apples, roughly chopped with skin on but core removed
Juice of a small Lemon, about 30ml

Method:

Put a cup of dandelion petals to one side. Place the rest of the ingredients in a large saucepan on a low heat, and stir regularly until the sugar is dissolved. Turn up and bring to the boil, stirring regularly, and then turn down and simmer with the lid on for about 20 minutes. Check on the mixture and stir frequently. The apples should have softened. If not leave for another 5 minutes until they have softened, and remove from the heat.

Mash the mixture together and then leave the mixture to stand and cool for at least 30 minutes.

Strain the mixture through a muslin sheet.

Measure the mixture. You should have about 3 cups of fluid. If not, add a little water. Return the liquid to a clean saucepan, and add the extra cup of dandelion flowers. Gently bring to the boil, without a lid, stirring regularly. Then lower to a rolling boil (roiling boil) i.e. boiling rapidly with lots of bubbling. Do not let the mixture boil over, so keep and eye on the pan and stir frequently.

After about 20-25 minutes, test for the setting point on a thermometer. If you don't have a jam thermometer, you can do this by freezing a small plate for 20-25 minutes and placing a small spoonful of hot jam on the plate. Leave for a few minutes, then draw a line through the jam with the tip of your finger. If it wrinkles a bit and does not flow easily back into the gap it's ready.

Once at setting point, if necessary, remove any frothy scum from the top of the mixture, and pour the marmalade into sterilised jars. If needed, gently stir marmalade to ensure an even distribution of petals. Close the jars and allow to set.

Fuchsia Flower Jelly

Ingredients:
2- 4 cups Fuchsia flowers
2 cups granulated Sugar and also
4 cups granulated Sugar
1/2 cup Lemon juice
6 cups Water
125ml Apple Pectin

Method:
Gently wash the Fuchsia, remove the pistil and stamen and any green/ brown discolouration at the foot of flower.

Place the flowers in a bowl with 2 cups of sugar and the lemon juice. With one hand, begin to massage the sugar and juice into the petals. The petals will start to wilt, and after a few minutes, stir and you should have a pink syrupy paste.

Next, combine the water, half of the pectin and 4 cups sugar in a pot. Place over med/high heat and stir until the sugar dissolves. Bring to a boil and then add the fuchsia petal mixture. Stir fuchsia into the boiling water. Let the Fuchsia simmer over medium/high heat for about 30-40 minutes. Add the rest of the pectin and stir regularly for another 10 minutes. If using a jam thermometer, cook the jam until it reaches 110°C. Test for setting on frozen plate. At that point, remove from heat and pour into sterilised jars. Allow to cool at room temperature.

Fuchsia Berry Jam

Ingredients:
450g granulated Sugar
2 tablespoons (30ml) Apple Pectin
Juice of 1 Lemon
680g Fuchsia Berries

Method:
Place the sugar, pectin and lemon juice in a saucepan and heat slowly, stirring frequently, until the sugar has dissolved. Allow the mixture to cool and gently stir the berries into the mixture. Slowly bring the mixture to the boil on a medium heat. Simmer until the setting point is reached. If using a jam thermometer, cook jam until it reaches 110°C or test for setting on a frozen plate. At that point, remove from the heat and pour into sterilised jars. Allow to cool at room temperature.

Dandelion Muffins

Makes about 6 small muffins

Ingredients:
88g Self-Raising Flour
35g Margarine
30g granulated Sugar
Half a Tablespoon Honey or Syrup (Clover, Gorse or Honeysuckle Syrup are recommended)
75ml Milk
10g Dandelion petals (Remove as much of the surrounding green as possible)
¼ Teaspoon of ground Black Pepper

Method:
Place the margarine, sugar, black pepper and honey or syrup in a large bowl, and cream until well combined. Gradually stir in the milk and sifted flour, a little at a time, until the mix is smooth. Mix in the Dandelion petals until all the ingredients are evenly combined.
Pre-heat fan oven to 200°C. Transfer the mixture to cupcake cases and place on a cupcake tray, and place in the centre of the oven for about 12-15 minutes, until they have risen and are a golden brown colour.

Lavender Cupcakes

Makes 6 small cupcakes

To Make Lavender Water:
Place quarter of a teaspoon of dried Lavender flowers in a small container (shot glass works) and pour over a teaspoon of boiling water. Stir, and cover so that steam does not escape. Leave to soak for at least an hour, and once cooled can be left overnight in the fridge.

Ingredients:
70g Margarine
70g granulated Sugar
70g Self-Raising Flour
1 Egg
1 teaspoon Lavender Water
1 teaspoon dried Lavender flowers

Method:
Combine the margarine and sugar in a large bowl, and cream together until thoroughly mixed. Add the egg and sifted flour and stir until the mixture is smooth. Add in the lavender water and lavender flowers and stir until evenly distributed.
Preheat oven to 180°C. Place the mixture in cupcake cases and onto a cupcake tray, and bake in the middle of the oven for 20 minutes, until they have risen and are golden brown on top.

Rose & Black Pepper Muffins

Makes approximately 12 small muffins

Ingredients:
180g Self-Raising Flour
80g Margarine
70g granulated Sugar
2 tablespoons Lemon juice
(about 1 lemon)
150ml Milk
60g fresh fragrant Rose petals
¼ teaspoon of ground Black Pepper

Method:
Place the rose petals in a bowl and stir in the lemon juice for a few minutes until the petals are covered. Leave for a few minutes and stir in the sugar. Stir until all the petals are thoroughly coated. Cover, and leave for at least an hour. If leaving overnight, put the bowl in the fridge.
Combine the margarine and black pepper in a large bowl, and cream until well combined. Gradually stir in the milk and sifted flour, a little at a time, until it's all smoothly combined. Use a hand blender to break up the petal mixture and then add it to the bowl, making sure as much rose juice goes in as possible, with the rest of the ingredients, and stir until everything is evenly combined.
Pre-heat fan oven to 200°C. Transfer the mixture to cupcake cases and on to a cupcake tray, leaving a bit of room for the muffins to rise. Place in the middle of the oven for about 15-18 minutes or until they have risen and are a golden brown colour, and firm yet bouncy on top. Leave to cool before consuming.

Flower Power Lemon Cheesecake

We've used Pansies, but you can try this recipe with different edible flowers throughout the seasons!

Ingredients
250g Digestive Biscuits
100g Butter, melted
650g Soft Cheese
120g Icing Sugar
20g Pansy petals
30ml Lemon juice
284ml Double Cream

Method:
To make the base, butter or line a 23cm loose-bottomed tin with baking parchment. Put the digestive biscuits in a bowl and crush to crumbs, then pour over the melted butter. Mix thoroughly until the crumbs are completely coated. Place them into the prepared tin, and firmly press down into the base to create an even layer. Put in the fridge for 1 hour, until the base is set firmly.

Place the clean petals and sugar into a bowl and add the lemon juice. Stir thoroughly until mixed and the colour of the sugar starts changing, and leave for an hour or until the biscuit base is ready.

Add the soft cheese into the bowl of pansy sugar paste, and beat with an electric hand mixer until smooth. Pour in the double cream and continue beating until the mixture is completely combined. Spoon the cream mixture onto the biscuit base, then smooth the top of the cheesecake down with the back of a spatula. Leave to set in the fridge overnight.

Bring the cheesecake to room temperature about 30 minutes before serving. Decorate with some fresh or candied flowers.

Candied Flowers

Ingredients:
Edible flowers (depending on the quantity you would like to make)
Icing Sugar (dependent on the number of flowers)
1 Egg white

Method:
Use clean, dry edible flowers such as, viola, pansies, dahlias, carnations and roses. Use either the petals or cut the flowers as close to the base as possible if using whole.

Whisk an egg white in a bowl until white and frothy, and with a small pastry or clean paint brush completely cover the petals or flower. Tweezers are really helpful to hold the flowers, as they get slippery.

Coat with a fine dusting of icing sugar over both sides. If the sugar is absorbed after five minutes, cover with more icing sugar, then shake off any excess. Tweezers are particularly helpful at this stage, to keep hands clean.

Place the covered flowers or petals on greasproof paper, lined with a fine layer of icing sugar, to dry at room temperature for a minimum of twelve hours.

Flowers are completely dry when stiff to the touch. Store in an airtight container, separated by tissue paper, or covered in a good dusting of icing sugar, out of direct sunlight at room temperature.

Apple & Daisy Crumble

Ingredients:
70g granulated Sugar
20g fresh Daisies (40g frozen or half a cup)
3 tablespoons (45ml) of Water
1 tablespoon Cornflour (or Plain Flour)
227g Crumble Mix
450g Apples (3-4 large), peeled, cored and diced into 2 cm cubes

Method:
Place the sugar and daisies in a saucepan and add the water. Gently heat, stirring well to dissolve the sugar. Once the mixture has started to boil, turn off heat, cover and leave for at least 1 hour.

Grease a 1 litre oven proof dish with butter or margarine, and layer the apples on the bottom.

Add the cornflour to the sugar and daisy mix and stir into a smooth paste. Cover the apples evenly with the mixture. Then cover all with the crumble mix.

Cook in a pre-heated fan oven at 180°C for about 45 minutes, until the crumble has browned on top and the apple and daisy mixture is bubbling.

Gardener's Tonic

Ingredients:

1 litre Vodka (medium range quality is fine)
1 tablespoon dry young Nettle leaves, dried. To add a green tea quality
1 tablespoon dry Clover leaves, dried. For a hint of vanilla
1 tablespoon Daisy flowers, dried. For a herbal flavour
1 tablespoon or 10 leaves of Lemon Balm, dried. To add a citrus note
2 tablespoons Pansy petals, dried. For some colour and floral flavour
1 teaspoon Lavender flowers, dried. To add a perfume

Method:

Add all the ingredients into a clean air-tight glass jar. Close the jar and shake ingredients together for about 60 seconds. Place in a dark, cool place. Shake and check daily. The mix should be ready after 7 days. However, after 3 days, you can taste daily before shaking to see whether you're happy with the flavour. Adjust if needed, by adding more ingredients to taste.

When you're happy with the flavour, strain the mixture through muslin, and pour into a clean, sterile bottle. Either the original bottle of vodka, or smaller gift bottles. Store in a cool, dark place, or keep cool in the fridge.

Serving Suggestion: Pour 35ml Gardener's Tonic into a glass with ice, and add 180ml of sparkling water

Elderflower Champagne

Ingredients:
6-8 heads of Elderflower
1 Lemon & 1 Lime
750g of granulated Sugar
2 tablespoons of Apple Cider Vinegar
5 litres of Water

Method:
Pick nice young flower heads and remove as much of the stem as possible. Just use the flowers if you have the patience to remove from the umbel.

Pour 5 litres of water into a large lidded saucepan or a bowl, which can then be covered with a tea towel. If it's a cold day you may want to heat the water slightly so the sugar will dissolve more readily.

Add the elderflower and a sliced lemon and a sliced lime.

Then add 750g of sugar and two tablespoons of cider vinegar and stir until all the sugar has dissolved.

Stir and cover, then leave it for 48 hours. Then check to see if fermentation has begun, with small bubbles forming in the mixture. If after 5 days, fermentation has not started, add some yeast. Champagne yeast ideally, but any yeast will kick start it. Then leave for a couple of days before checking again. Once it's started to ferment strain the liquid, ideally through a clean muslin cloth.

Then pour into bottles. Some prefer to use plastic bottles as they have more give, as glass bottles can explode as the mixture carbonates if left unchecked for a while.

After about 2 weeks it should be ready to drink. Ideally, it's best to drink it within 6 months, as it will strengthen and turn more into a wine/liqueur with age.

Cleavers Coffee

Ingredients & Method:

Collect the amount of seeds you want to make, about half a cup should be enough for a few brews.

Seperate the seeds out onto kitchen paper or a kitchen towel, and allow to dry in an area with plenty of warm air circulating.
You can either roast them gently in a medium hot, dry skillet or place on an oven tray and roast in the oven at 150°C for about 10 minutes ,or until they brown. Leave to cool a while, and they should have a strong coffee-type odour. Grind the seeds and store in an air-tight container.
To make cleavers coffee: add about 1 tablespoon of the cleavers coffee to a measuring cup of boiling water and leave steep for 5-10 minutes, and then strain before serving. Add honey or syrup to sweeten. Try adding different flavours to the brew such as ginger, spices or other herbs.

Dandelion Coffee

Ingredients & Method:
Approximately 12-16 roots makes enough for a cup of non-caffeinated dandelion 'coffee'.

Dig up a large bunch of dandelion roots, remember they can go very deep, so it's best to get a large fork to to loosen the soil around the root, to get as much of it out as possible intact. After gathering the roots, clean them as best as you can. Remove any straggly, very thin parts from the roots. Tie the roots individually with a piece of string and hang them somewhere dry, with plently of airflow. Leave them to air dry until brittle, which should be within 2 weeks. Once dry, cut them into smaller pieces.
The dried roots can be kept in an air tight jar or container, and used to make teas, or added to flavour foods. However, to make a 'coffee', arrange the root pieces onto an oven tray and roast the dandelion root at 90°C for about 30-40 minutes, until the roots are brown and dried right through, but not burnt. Once the roots have cooled, grind them up and return to the tray and oven at about 80°C for another 5 minutes. Store the dandelion 'coffee' in an airtight container.
To use as a hot beverage: add about 2-3 tablespoons of dandelion 'coffee' to 2 cups of boiling water and simmer on low, with the lid on, for 10-15 minutes. Try experimenting by adding different spices or herbs to the brew. Strain and serve, you can add honey, syrup or milk to taste.
Dandelion 'coffee' can also be used to add flavour to soups, casseroles, curries and other dishes.

Gardener's Face Toner

The beauty product you can dilute in your drink or drizzle over salad!

Ingredients & Method:
Plants can be fresh or dried.

Pour 1 cup of (ideally distilled) boiling Water over a mixture of:
1.5 teaspoons of Rose petals – which are said to have anti-inflammatory and antioxidant properties.
1.5 teaspoons of Lavender flowers – which are meant to be beneficial for acne and have anti-inflammatory and antiseptic properties.
1.5 teaspoons of Sage leaves – these are said to have antiseptic, antibiotic, anti-fungal and astringent properties.
1.5 teaspoons of Rosemary leaves – which are said to have astringent, disinfectant, and antioxidant properties.

Cover, so the steam can't escape. It's best to use a jar or air-tight container, and steep (for at least 30-60 minutes but ideally leave overnight) and strain.

Optional: Add 1 to 5 ratio of apple cider vinegar to herbal water – which is used as a natural exfoliant and for antibacterial properties.
Best stored in a sealed bottle in the fridge.
To use, simply dampen some cotton wool with the toner and wipe over the face. There is no need to rinse.

Printed in Great Britain
by Amazon